Sally C

NAKED
IN WINTER

BEING A VERY DEDICATED IF
SOMETIMES CHILLY NATURIST

DEDICATED, WITH LOVE, TO
BRYAN
THANK YOU FOR BEING MY FRIEND

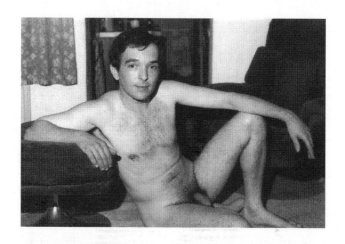

© COPYRIGHT 2014
PURPLE PANTHER PUBLISHING
ALL RIGHTS RESERVED

ONE

It is very easy for someone to be a naturist or a nudist or simply to take all their clothes off in the warmth of the summer sun. The really dedicated naturist longs to be naked in all seasons, not all the time but in those moments when the desire to experience the freedom of being naked is simply irresistible, no matter what the weather - such as now, for instance.

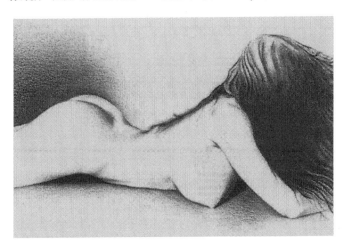

Actually, I must be honest and admit that I am cheating a little bit. I am not completely naked. I am wearing a pair of thick cotton ankle socks - grey ones. It is not all that cold today but my little feet are feeling chilly and if there is something I cannot bear it is cold feet. When I first discovered naturism as a teenager, I began to sleep in the nude no matter what the weather was like. But in the past few years - especially when I have been in my native England - I find that a nice pair of bed socks helps to keep me cosy and warm under the duvet. And they are a life saver if I have to make a mad dash to the loo in the middle of the night. It may look silly but it is all part of being slightly eccentric.

I really do not like winter and I am not particularly fond of autumn either, especially October - so many of the rotten things that have happened to me in my life have happened in October. I used to wish that I could just hibernate for six months of the year but then I moved from England to France where the climate is marginally better. The trouble is that, for one reason or another, I find myself returning to England at regular intervals and it is almost always cold, wet and dreary when I get there. It is not easy to be a naturist in England at the best of times but somehow I have managed it. You should see the heating bills from my old house.

It would be wonderful, in an ideal world, to simply follow the sun throughout the year, going from one warm place to another. If I ever win the lottery, I will probably do that but for the time being I shall just have to muddle through as best I can - being naked with socks on when the moment is right. In my little villa in the naturist resort of Montavilet I can spend most of the day without clothes. When the sun goes down, I have a choice of apparel. I can either wear a short, silky kimono-type dressing gown that has a hint of elegance or a big, long fluffy bathrobe that is as cosy and comfortable as an embrace. Either way, I can be naked underneath – at least until I go to England again.

I share the villa with a slightly older French woman named Sabine who is not exactly a natural naturist. When she is indoors, she almost always wears at least knickers and shoes. Mind you, if I had her collection of knickers I would probably want to show them off too. I have never seen such an extensive range of sexy, dark-coloured underwear. I sometimes wonder if she ever wears the same pair of knickers twice and yet she seems to regard me as eccentric for wanting to be naked as much as possible. We are about to share our first winter together and it will be interesting to see how she adapts to the change of season. No doubt she will be covering up more than me but I would be willing to bet that she has a pair or two of fur-lined panties. Well, I have got my own fur down there.

My body is still in quite good shape for someone who is now closer to forty than to thirty which is amazing considering that my only forms of exercise are walking and swimming. But being a naturist is not merely an act of exhibitionism although I will admit that I like the occasional appreciate glance. For me, being naked is all about freedom and feeling a part of nature. As the weather turns cool and the days become increasingly shorter, I am reluctant to put clothes on while I wait impatiently for the arrival of spring.

The simple fact is that I need the sun. I am sure that I suffer from seasonal affective disorder. Anyone who knows me will attest that my mood is primarily dictated by the presence or absence of the sun. I would love to someday go to somewhere like St. Petersburg where they have the white nights in summer when the sun virtually never sets. But I would have to be well away before the oppesite happened - those months when there is next to no sunlight at all. That would drive me insane. I cannot understand how anyone, except possibly vampires, could live in such conditions. The cold weather is bad enough but at least let me have some sunlight.

Years ago, one of my ex-husbands and I spent Christmas with some friends in their villa in Lanzarote. It was the first time I had ever experienced Christmas in a warm climate. The four of us were naked except for Santa hats and we all laughed when someone would receive an item of clothing as a present. Our host made certain there was mistletoe hung in places that were difficult to avoid. I actually had a swim in the pool on Christmas Day. It was marvellous but it certainly did not feel anything like Christmas – sitting around a piano and singing *White Christmas* in that setting was just weird. And yet that is what I had wanted, or thought I wanted – to escape from the English winter at least temporarily. Sometimes being warm and naked is not enough.

My favourite Christmas card

No doubt I will be spending this coming Christmas in England – spending time with my family in Hampshire and visiting one or two dear friends who live nearby – and the opportunities for nudity will probably be limited to the shower and to bed. When I had my own house in Hampshire it was quite possible to be at least a part-time indoor naturist thanks to the fireplace in the sitting room. I was able to read books, watch telly, play my piano, and even entertain a guest or two in a very warm and relaxed environment. I could see the winter through the window and smile at it from my own little cosy oasis. Winter nudists are invariably indoor nudists but there are a few brave souls who actually venture outside in the nearly altogether.

Some years ago, on a very memorable summer holiday in Croatia, I met a charming Russian couple named Olga and Vyacheslav with whom I managed to communicate in French. They were very dedicated naturists who lived on the western fringe of Siberia. We exchanged letters for about a year and they once sent me a photograph of the very beautiful Olga out in the snow wearing nothing but a pair of big boots. I was absolutely amazed - why would she even want to do that? It was true dedication. I got shivers just looking at the picture but I was intrigued by how happy she seemed. In the spirit of "I'll try anything once", I decided to give it a go the next time we had snow in Hampshire which, fortunately, does not happen very often.

As it turned out, that January we had more snow than usual - a heavy blanket of the white stuff covered the fields and clung to the trees and actually looked quite beautiful when viewed from the inside the house. I looked at the snow glistening in the late morning sunlight, remembered Olga's happy expression from her photograph, and felt a strange compulsion to take my clothes off and go outside. When I had finally worked up the courage to do so, I was not completely naked. In addition to my furry boots, I wore a woolly hat with matching mittens and a scarf. I must have looked a sight but luckily there was no one around to see me - or to talk me out of it.

I stood by the kitchen door for about five minutes. I could feel the chilly draught as a light wind gently blew the snow about. After momentarily questioning my sanity, I opened the door and stepped out into the paved courtyard behind my house. As I moved towards the nearby field, the snow became deeper. It was not even a foot deep but that was a lot for Hampshire. The initial shock of the cold soon gave way to a kind of numbness - the one thing I was vividly aware of was the effect on my nipples which caused me to wonder about the possibility of icicles forming on my nether regions. I was bloody cold. I took a couple of more steps, paused then retreated as quickly as I could back into the house. I stood in front of the fireplace as I waited for the kettle to boil then had a huge mug of tea. I took off my boots and woolly bits, put on slippers and a fleecy dressing gown, and sat in front of the fire and called myself a variety of names that questioned my intelligence and also included a couple of unkind words for Olga. That was my first and only experiment with being naked in the snow.

Serpentine swimmers

There are obviously some people who can stand the cold better than others – and not just in wintry places like Russia and Scandinavia. Every year on Christmas Day, hundreds of people go for a swim in the icy waters of the Serpentine in London's Hyde Park. Of course, they are not naked but they might just as well be. Being cold is bad enough but cold and wet? The only way I would do that is in a place like Lanzarote or perhaps in a heated indoor swimming pool in a nice hotel like the Hotel New York in Disneyland Paris where I once spent several rather strange and somewhat naughty days with a potential soul mate. The only problem was that I had to wear a bikini – top and bottom! Well, I didn't want to frighten the children.

I sometimes think that if I had stayed in Hampshire I might have eventually got a hot tub. They seem to be all the rage in England at the moment for some reason. I think I could manage a naked dash from the house to the tub knowing that the destination was worthwhile. And one of the nice things about hot tubs - so I have been told - is that they are big enough to share with friends.

Of course, one of the best ways to keep warm during winter is to cuddle with someone who likes you as much as you like them. Naturally, naked cuddles are the best. As I have said on many occasions, one of the most enjoyable aspects of naturism - no matter what the season - is its sensuality. There are some urists among the naturist movement who like to pretend that sex has nothing to do with naturism but they are only fooling themselves. Sex is definitely a part of it. It is not the most important part of it but it is always there - lurking somewhere beneath the surface. At least, that has been my experience. But, just like nudity, sex somehow seems less of an issue during the winter months - or maybe that's just me.

===

TWO

So the weather turns chilly and the logical place to be naked is indoors. Even without the summer sun, there is that wonderful feeling of freedom that comes from not wearing clothes. The heating is increased and the nudity only lasts an hour or two at a time but otherwise things are much the same. The whole point of naturism is to carry on with everyday things while being naked. That includes mundane things like housework although I have never been very good at that - clothed or not. I really hate all that dusting and polishing and hoovering. Once it is done, it just has to be done all over again six months later. The one concession I make is that I always wear an apron when cooking, especially if I am frying or grilling. No point in tempting fate and more than one guest has commented about how nice my exposed bum looks when I am wearing my apron.

Naked scrubber

The first hint that I may need to put some clothes on is usually a sneeze. One of the few drawbacks of nudity is that there is no place to carry a tissue or a hankie. Another side effect of being chilly is that my nipples seem to be permanently erect which is not necessarily an unpleasant sensation. Some of my male friends tell me that they dislike the cold because it produces what might be politely described as "shrinkage". Perhaps that is why my gay friend Bryan decided to move to California.

One of my favourite indoor activities is playing the piano. I can lose myself in music for hours at a time. Sabine tells me that I sometimes hum quietly as I am playing which is something I had never been aware of. I would love to give a recital in the nude but can never decide if the audience should be naked as well.

Everybody loves music. My parents' generation was well known for smoking pot while listening to music – they still do for all I know – but I love to be naked both when playing and listening. My dear friend Fleur, who had been a professional dancer, was absolutely magical when she used to dance naked around my sitting room as I played Chopin or Debussy. When I occasionally had naturist parties, we played CDs of more modern music and the sight of naked couples dancing together was heart-warming. One of these days, I must learn how to tango. I will need very sexy shoes for that but nothing else.

While I spend the winter impatiently awaiting the return of the summer sun, there are some people who never venture outside naked no matter what the weather is and who prefer to be strictly indoor naturists in the privacy and security of their own homes. Perhaps they lack the self-confidence to be naked where they might be seen. Sometimes they are such secret naturists that they only strip off when they are alone and even their spouses are unaware of their predilection for nudity. No one ever sees them naked which I find rather sad because naturism really is much better when it is a shared experience. But I suppose that people find their sense of joy in all sorts of ways.

Of course, living in a naturist resort makes that sort of thing much easier but even when I lived in straight-laced Hampshire I was never overly worried about being seen naked.

"GEE, USUALLY JEHOVA'S WITNESSES STICK AROUND AND CHAT LONGER..."

It must be nice to live in a city that has organised naturist events to enjoy an activity among other like-minded naked people although I would be hesitant to join a naked bike ride. I would not mind the exercise or being seen and even filmed naked but the prospect of my little bum on one of those thin hard bike saddles almost brings tears to my eyes.

A much more appealing proposition is when cultural institutions occasionally have a naturist or clothes optional day. Apparently there had been such a day at an art museum in Vienna where throngs of nudists were allowed to wander through the galleries to admire and enjoy the various works of arts and, possibly, each other. It seems such a perfect combination - art and nudity. After all, the nude has been one of the most popular art forms ever since the days of cave drawings. I would absolutely love an opportunity like that. I could just imagine the thrill of being naked in places like the Van Gogh Museum in Amsterdam or Musee d'Orsay in Paris (my all-time favourite museum). I would even consider taking my clothes off for the Tate in London although I suspect hell will freeze over first.

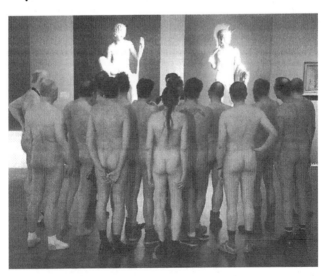

I have always wanted to pose naked for a truly talented painter or photographer, either on my own or with others. I could imagine myself in all sorts of poses, one or two of which might be considered slightly pornographic. Well, art and beauty are in the eye of the beholder. A lot of people have seen my naked body but I am unsure how many of them would consider it a work of art.

A few years ago, I saw a fascinating television documentary about a performance artist named Marina Abramovic and a show she was doing at the Museum of Modern Art in New York. A lot of her work had involved nudity and there were a number of nude models with her for this show although she herself remained clothed. Her performance was to sit silently at a table. People took turns sitting opposite her and staring at her for a couple of minutes. This went on for hours every day and produced all sorts of results. It all seemed very strange.

In order to enter the exhibition, everyone had to pass through a very narrow doorway. This was made even narrower by a pair of very still and very naked models. The only way in was to squeeze between them – it was impossible not to have contact with them. I thought that was a brilliant idea – I really wish I could have been there. I wondered if I would have had the nerve to be one of the models. There were other live naked "exhibits" as well. The only problem was that when a member of the audience decided to join in the spirit of the occasion by taking his clothes off, he was swiftly bundled away by the security guards which was a shame because if ever there was an art exhibition for naked patrons, that was it.

It seems a ridiculous paradox that many people will go to museums and art galleries to gaze intently at paintings and sculptures of nudes yet would be horrified to encounter a naked person in the flesh. What is the difference? What are they afraid of? No one is asking them to undress - unless they wander into a naturist resort or beach and then they are on my turf. I am not a naturist missionary - I am not trying to convince other people to strip. I merely wish to make my own choice about wearing clothes or not. And I would love to have the blissful freedom to be naked and surrounded by art.

Unfortunately, such possibilities at the moment are only pipe dreams. My piano and my laptop are my primary sources of culture - that and listening to Sabine who is very intelligent and very serious. Sometimes I catch her looking at me and I wonder what she is thinking. Hopefully, not that my bum is looking big.

==

THREE

One of my great pleasures – in any weather – has always been reading. My house used to be littered with stacks of books everywhere – all sorts of books from the complete works of Terry Pratchett to various histories and biographies and even an occasional volume of popular philosophy. But I never encountered very many books about naturism until I got my first Kindle reader. It was then I realised just how popular a subject nudity was although I have no idea why I should have been surprised. Of course, the best way to read about being naked is to be naked yourself.

I was more than a little disappointed to discover that many of these so-called naturist books were not really about naturism at all – not real naturism. Yes, they had nudity in them but nudity is not the same thing as naturism. Many of the books were basically pornography. Now I have nothing against pornography as such but I do expect it to at least be well written. Some of the books I found read like teenage wet dreams with numerous typos and terrible grammar. Serious editing was needed.

There were some interesting and even delightful naturist books – *Nice Girls Can Be Nudists Too* by Liz Egger being an excellent example. But too many were simply badly constructed sex stories with cardboard characters or fictionalised accounts by alleged naturists who probably never went naked in public in their life. Needless to say, I deleted most of those books without finishing them. I can only hope that some of their readers do not get the wrong impression of what naturism is really like.

In some of the books, being naked was actually regarded as a form of punishment. One particularly depressing story was about a woman whose husband had convinced her to be naked in the middle of a big city for an entire day. The premise was, of course, totally unrealistic but it might have made for a reasonably nice fantasy if the author had not given it a somewhat nasty turn. Another book had a young chap moving into a house with three girls who, they announced happily, were naturists who preferred to be naked indoors and expected him to do the same. This really was in the realms of fantasy. It might have worked as an exploration of the freedom of naturism but instead it was just another sex story – the girls were not so much naturists as sex kittens.

Some people obviously enjoy these sorts of stories. I only wish they were not presented as naturist books. I am the first to admit that it is not always possible to separate sex from being naked but I also believe that being naked is an experience in itself. I may occasionally stray into brief accounts about my love life that has resulted from naturism but I do not take my clothes off simply because I am looking for someone to go to bed with. Well, maybe once or twice but sex is not my primary motive for wanting to be naked.

In looking through the books on offer, I came across a slightly strange phenomenon that I had not previously been aware of. It was a series of stories about CFNM – clothed female, nude male. I have been in situations where some people are naked while others are fully clothed but this seemed to be a deliberate arrangement in which the naked male was taken advantage of.

Personally, I would prefer it the other way around. I can remember a time when I was still with my second husband when I was naked in the house while he and his mate were not. It was on a crisp autumn evening but we had the fire going. I was not trying to be particularly provocative. I had been naked when the two of them arrived home from the pub and I saw no reason why I should cover myself up for them in my own home. The other bloke obviously enjoyed the view but there was nothing said - at least not in my presence - and nothing improper attempted. They could have stripped off if they wanted to but they obviously did not want to. The situation had nothing to do with sex - I was merely being comfortable. If I remember correctly, my husband's friend was always very nice to me afterwards.

I really should not complain about the books available on Kindle because Kindle has been very good to me both as a writer and a reader. I have grown quite fond of my little Paperwhite and it has certainly helped to save on space in my villa, not to mention being very handy when I travel. Sorry if this sounds like an advert but writing these little books has been a wonderful creative outlet for me and without being able to self-publish them there would not be much point to writing them. It is interesting that my books are also available in paperback form but the Kindle versions outsell them by a wide margin. I would hate to think that real books are becoming obsolete.

Sabine, who shares my villa, also loves books but she is deeply suspicious of innovations such as Kindle. She prefers real books and most of hers of heavy hardback books about history - all in French. She is working on a lengthy historical novel about Pauline Bonaparte - I doubt there is a single humorous line in it. Sabine is so serious and old-fashioned in many ways that I am surprised that she is writing her book on a computer rather than scratching it out on paper with a quill pen.

Sabine is so quirky that it is impossible to dislike her. One evening, we were looking for something to watch on television - a rare event in itself - when we came across a French film featuring a very well-known actress. Sabine refused to watch it because she was of the opinion that actress always gave the impression of having dirty feet. You cannot argue with a prejudice like that.

I doubt that I will see very much of Sabine's well preserved body during the winter - perhaps if I turn the heating in the villa up high enough. She certainly thinks I am eccentric for wanting to be naked in cold weather. Maybe one day she will read one of my books and understand why I am the way I am.

Even my cat Mittens seems furrier in the winter months. I suppose it is all a case of being able to adapt. Perhaps I should let my hair grow and stop shaving my legs. No, that would be a step too far. Maybe instead I could persuade Mittens to help keep me warm.

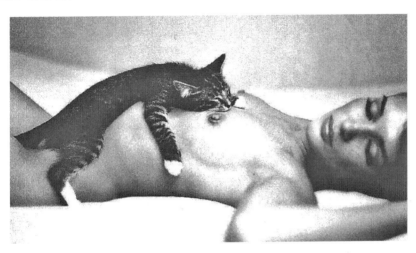

One thing that would certainly enliven the cooler season would be the occasional visitor. The population of Montavilet becomes sparse once the temperature begins to drop. Friends and family sometimes stop by, usually when they are on their way to somewhere else. My old friend Maggie and her new husband came for a quick visit last November. They had been in Paris and Maggie decided that she wanted to see me. We were once very close but had somehow lost touch. Not knowing what her husband Ian was like, I put on some clothes to welcome them to my villa which, for that night, I had all to myself.

The visit seemed overly polite. Married life obviously agreed with Maggie but she had changed a lot. Her husband was pleasant enough, if a little quiet, and seemed to be making a special effort to look at my face and not my covered body. I was half tempted to strip off just to see what sort of reaction I would get. I had a few precious moments alone with Maggie in the kitchen and then - just briefly - everything was the way it used to be between us. Maggie also thanked me for being dressed. Ian apparently knew that I was a naturist but Maggie did not feel he needed a demonstration. I actually felt a little bit hurt by that. After they left, I could not wait to be naked again.

Marriage has a strange effect on some people. I know - I have been married and divorced twice. Encountering naturists can also have a strange effect on those people we naked people refer to as textiles. I wish it would have been warmer when Maggie and Ian visited. I would gladly have been naked and Ian would have just had to deal with it. I can only wonder if he knew that Maggie and I used to be naked together. I hope I never reach the point of being even slightly ashamed or embarrassed about being a naturist. You can look at my body or not - the choice is yours. But it is my decision whether I am naked or not. And right now I am naked.

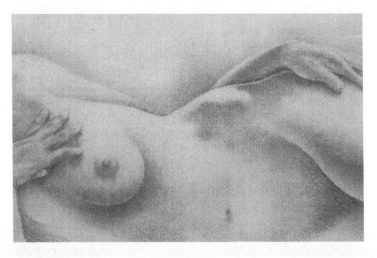

I hope it is not going to me a long winter because my poor little nipples feel like ice.

==

FOUR

It is interesting how, in recent years, nudity or at least toplessness has become an instrument of protest. I suppose the naked body - in particular the naked female body - has been used to draw attention to all sorts of causes. I wonder if the suffragettes ever considered a "burn your corset" campaign or if women could get equal pay with men simply by taking their tits out. Of course, by the Sixties naked female breasts were a common sight at anti-war demonstrations as indeed they were, along with total nudity, at music festivals. These women were not necessarily naturists but they understood the impact a pair of boobs had on the mass media. Now, with the internet, that impact can be felt much farther even if many of the viewers have little or no interest in the cause being espoused.

Topless politics has come to prominence from, of all places, some Arabic countries with the rise of Femen - women protesting their treatment and lack of rights by publicly displaying various slogans across their bare bosoms. They often paid a heavy price for such boldness but their cause was enthusiastically taken on by their spiritual sisters in other parts of the world, especially in some of the big cities of the West. It was there that the freedom of expression and supposedly indecent exposure clashed to produce the jackpot of fantastic photo opportunities. It was hardly naturism as we know it but it was very brave.

It was hard to determine if the Powers That Be were upset that women were acting so politically or whether they were doing it so sexually. I will bare my breasts at the drop of a hat but I had never considered emblazoning them with any sort of message. I suppose I do possess some prime advertising space although I hope we never reach the point where bodies are used for such commercial purposes. Apparently in Japan there was an instance where young girls in short skirts were paid to have advertising printed on their thighs. I can only wonder – what next?

The original Femen girls met very heavy opposition. It is not easy being a woman in a Muslim country at the best of times. There is such a difference in attitudes that it is hard to comprehend. I went to Tunisia on holiday once. They tolerated Western women in bikinis and even being topless on some of the tourist beaches but unless you were accompanied by a very strong man you could expect to be constantly pestered by the local yokels who apparently considered all Western women to be little better than whores.

I consider myself fairly liberal and open-minded but I cannot think of any cause that I would risk getting arrested for except possibly the closing of some beloved naturist facility which, these days, is ever a possibility. While I greatly admire all those half-naked girls making their loud and colourful protests, I am afraid that I am a little too much of a coward to join them - maybe when I was younger and more reckless. But now I seem to have achieved some measure of maturity even though I was not looking for it. I would really hate to be arrested at some protest and have some policeman point at one of the other girls and ask me: "Is this your daughter?" I mean, bloody hell, I'm only thirty-seven!

Luckily, not all of the topless protests are political. The one that I am especially fond of at the moment is the Free The Nipple campaign. This seems to be a largely American movement where women wish to have the same right as men to go topless in warm weather, not just on the beach but on the street or anywhere else they want to. As someone who always went topless on the beach - even before I was a naturist - I can well understand their desire.

Unfortunately, America can be a very puritanical place when it comes to things like female nipples. Often when protesting, the women are topless but their nipples are covered with tape. For some reason, the authorities regard a bare breast with a covered nipple as much less threatening than a bare breast with a nipple – as if breasts could ever be threatening or even offensive. I always regarded female breasts as the friendliest part of the human anatomy and, to paraphrase someone from long ago, I never met a breast I did not like.

Some clever person has designed a flesh-coloured bikini top with painted on nipples that, when worn, makes the wearer appear topless. I thought about ordering one – just to show my solidarity – but then I realised I can be topless for real anytime I want, even in winter. I hope the Free The Nipple women achieve some sort of success. They – and nipples – deserve it.

I am glad that I live in a society where nipples have always been more or less free. I recently watched an old movie from the Seventies in which none of the women seemed to wear a bra and their nipples were very obvious beneath their clothing. For some reason, girls today seem to prefer bras. I hate movies where a couple are making passionate love yet the girl never takes her bra off and the guy never tries to. Why? Breasts are fun.

Once or twice, I have met someone who asked me, since I was a naturist, was I also a pagan. It seemed an odd question until I gave it some thought one evening while staring into the fire with my third glass of wine. Part of my enjoyment of naturism is feeling a part of nature and that seems to be one of the things which pagans do - at least, the new age pagans that seem to be growing in numbers back in England. I have never been a religious person but I can relate to some of the Old Ways, especially when it comes to being naked.

A pagan girl was once confronted by a very strait-laced Church of England-type woman who obviously thought - wrongly - that all pagans were devil worshippers. The girl gently told the woman that the two of them were not all that different. "You pray," she said, "I dance naked in the forest." There is not much you can say to that.

Most people know about the Druids and other pagans gathering at Stonehenge for the dawn of the Summer Solstice. Sadly, naked dancing does not seem to be allowed. But there is also a similar though less attended ceremony to mark the Winter Solstice. In fact, it is often claimed that the Christians stole the date for Christmas to overshadow the pagan festival. But neither of them featured much nudity.

For many years, I lived less than a half hour's drive from the wonderful monument of Stonehenge yet I never once attended these ceremonies. I wish I had if only out of curiosity. There is so much history and tradition in England that it seems a shame to neglect or ignore it. Some people dismiss pagans as being crackpots or latter day hippies but there is much more to them than that. Perhaps on my next trip back to Salisbury I will try to find a coven to join. More than one person has told me that I would make a wonderful witch - at least, I think I heard them correctly.

Winter Solstice at Stonehenge

I have casually met a few pagans in my time but most of my information about them comes from books and television documentaries. I certainly loved the image of a circle of naked people holding hands and dancing around a huge bonfire - I could easily see myself doing that. I think I would probably be the sort of pagan known as a pantheist - someone who does not believe in a God as such but believes that everything in nature is divine. I remember feeling exactly that way when I was naked on an ancient Greek island.

Whether I could ever get into all the pagan chants and rituals is another matter. But I love their sense of humour. "Pagans have rites too" proclaims one of their banners. I think that the basic thing with pagans is that they want to return to a simpler way of life and simpler times - the Old Ways. That is probably impossible to achieve in this day and age but it is a nice ambition. While I do not understand or agree with all their beliefs, I will be more than happy to join in a naked dance around a bonfire anytime.

If nothing else, I would like to have a pagan funeral - actually a funeral with very little ceremony, no prayers, a recording of Faure's *Pavane* and possibly the singing of *Jerusalem* if only because I have always liked that hymn and it was one of the first things I ever learned to play on the piano. I want to lie naked with some flowers in a wicker coffin and be cremated. The only thing I have not decided is where I want my ashes to be scattered. Am I getting morbid or what?

==

F I V E

You may well be wondering what all of this has to do with being naked in winter. Well, I tend to do a lot of thinking during the winter months and my thoughts go off in all directions. So in this little book you are sharing some of the thoughts I have when I am naked in winter. If you were with me, we would probably have long rambling conversations until the early hours of a rather chilly morning.

I really miss my old fireplace. If you cannot feel the warmth of the summer sun on your naked body, a cosy little fire is quite possibly the next best thing. I used to keep that fire going all day during the winter and loved sitting beside it or curling up in front of it. Sometimes I wore clothes but often I did not. It was the perfect place to read or to daydream and it created a wonderful atmosphere for entertaining guests, either a special someone or a small group of friends. It is possible for people to enjoy being naked together without it turning into an orgy. But even on my own, the furry rug in front of the fireplace was my favourite spot in the house.

Now in Montavilet I have to make do with candles which are not quite the same thing. I occasionally burn some incense as well but only in my bedroom because it seems to make Sabine sneeze. Luckily, the winters in this part of France are not as dreary as those back in Hampshire – they certainly are a lot drier. Probably the most depressing aspect of the English climate is all the rain. Snow can at least look beautiful but rain is just yucky. Here winters are merely dull but thankfully seldom frigid. In the evenings, I can often mooch around the villa wearing just a big chunky jumper, a pair of socks, and nothing else.

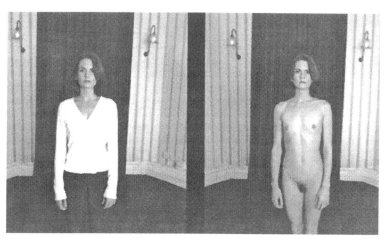

Honestly – which is nicer?

I made one of my return trips to England at the beginning of autumn. At least, the calendar said it was autumn but the country was enjoying an unusual spell of Indian summer – the sun was not only shining but it was warm. It was probably my only visit home in which I never once needed an umbrella. As usual, I spent only one night with my family in Hampshire before making my way to my preferred destination – the small but cosy flat of my very dear friend Fleur in Salisbury, a town for which I seem to develop more affection every time I go there. I suppose you sometimes have to leave a place to really appreciate it.

As always, it was wonderful to be reunited with Fleur who I absolutely love. Every time I see her, I try to convince her to come to Montavilet to live with me and every time she turns me down. Fleur is very much a romantic who still believes that she will find Mr. Right someday. Despite my best efforts, it never seems to occur to her that Mr. Right might possibly be Ms. Right. Either way, I am sure she could do better in France than in England but for Fleur that move would be a very big step.

When I arrived, Fleur had only recently ended yet another relationship and she was not in the most cheerful of moods. I did my best to make her smile and even persuaded her to do a little dance for me. Ballerina Fleur in motion is one of the most magical sights in the world.

It was warm enough for us to be naked in her flat and once our clothes were removed I realised how much I had missed Fleur. But she was more in the mood for comforting rather than affection. Still, no matter what the circumstances, a cuddle with Fleur is always a wonderful experience.

There were other compensations for returning to England. One thing that is impossible to find in France is a decent meal of fish and chips and I had been having a craving for that for weeks. In Salisbury, the best place for fish and chips is Stoby's on the Market Square and we ate there two nights in a row. It was worth getting dressed for a chance to devour a huge piece of plaice and a mountain of proper old-fashioned chips and some mushy peas. I really do have very simple tastes.

Stoby's fish and chips

Fleur was still trying to teach dance and music to children at one of the local schools and she appeared to be quite good at it. I once played the piano for one of her school recitals and I was amazed at how brilliantly she interacted with those little demons. I have never known how to deal with children - to me they have always been like alien beings from another world so it is just as well I never had any of my own. I even find it difficult to relate to the naturist kiddies at Montavilet, in particular the supposedly cute ones who make a habit of staring at my bits.

Years ago, I was quietly lying on a beach in Spain - a regular beach not a naturist one so I was merely topless - when a nearby English boy of about seven got up and called to his younger brother "Let's go see some tits!". The two of them went wandering along the beach with the older boy nonchalantly pointing out all the topless women to his somewhat overwhelmed sibling. After about fifteen minutes, they returned to their mother and proudly announced: "We've seen lots of tits!" at which point he cast his beady little eyes in my direction and I felt obliged to roll over onto my tummy. He was one of the very few males I ever encountered that I preferred not to expose my breasts to.

Back in Salisbury, Fleur and I took advantage of the pleasant weather for a leisurely stroll down to the Cathedral which I had not visited in years. It was, as always, impressive and I found myself wondering how blasphemous it would be to wander naked in such a place. Fleur was less than pleased that the stone floor was actually made up of slabs marking the final resting places of generations of the deceased. "We're walking on dead people," she kept whispering to me in the voice of someone who had obviously seen one too many horror films. It was a relief to get back out into the sun and to window shop on the way back to her flat where we were very happy to be naked again.

My previous visit to England had not been so pleasant - it was to attend the funeral of my Aunt Sophie, my father's rather free-spirited older sister. Sophie had been the wild one of her generation, a bit of a hippie as well as an eccentric non-conformist. She and I got along really well. My father told me that when she used to go to music festivals at places like Reading and Knebworth, she was one of the first to take her top off and to keep it off. Perhaps I inherited my love of naturism indirectly from her. She certainly always encouraged me to be myself and to not worry about what anyone else thought.

One of Aunt Sophie's self portraits

Sophie was a bit of an artist and was married three times before she finally found her soul mate. Unfortunately, he had a heart attack and died at the age of fifty and Sophie spent the rest of her life in a ramshackle cottage just outside Brentwood in Essex, a place once famous for burning witches. I used to love to visit her and she always encouraged me to take my clothes off if I wanted to. On one of my last visits, she gave me a small Art Deco figurine of an elegant nude that I had always admired. Sophie told me that she would have left it to me in her will - if she had ever got around to writing a will.

The funeral was a surprisingly traditional affair with prayers and hymns that the agnostic Sophie would have hated. I wish I had been able to play the organ for the service as I would have slipped in a couple of her beloved rock songs. As it was, I gave a reading of a couple of verses of Dylan Thomas's *Do Not Go Gentle Into That Good Night*. I remembered that Sophie had once told me that she could not decide who she liked more – Dylan Thomas or Bob Dylan. I always suspected that Sophie was a naturist at least in spirit. My father gave me some of her ashes to take back to France, a country she always loved.

Returning to Montavilet after a visit to England was always something of a culture shock. It is hard to believe that everything could be so different after travelling such a relatively short distance. It is a relief to be able to take my clothes off wherever I want to without anyone judging me. Even on a fairly balmy day, I stripped off as soon as I got out of the car for the short walk to the villa. I usually passed two or three other brave naked souls and we smiled at each other like the kindred spirits we were. At such moments, exposing my body to the elements was very much an assertion of my identity. Then I quickly went inside and had a big mug of hot chocolate.

It is always good to be home although sometimes the concept of home is difficult to define. There was an old saying that home is where you hang your hat. In my case, home is very much the place where I can feel totally relaxed and take my clothes off.

Luckily, I do not live either a lonely or a celibate existence, even in winter. I once shocked Sabine by returning home with a gentleman companion one night and a female friend the next. Being a naturist is all very well but sometimes the body indicates that it has certain needs or desires. I never had any particular aspirations for sainthood but I am hardly a super sinner either. I simply believe in following my instincts - a policy that has, shall we say, resulted in a fairly interesting life.

==

<u>S I X</u>

I worry about becoming a boring creature of habit. Every morning I wake up around 8am, have a quick shower then throw on a big fluffy robe as I stumble to the kitchen for the obligatory croissants and coffee. Consciousness gradually returns to my half-open eyes as they try to focus on what the world looks like on the other side of the window. Once breakfast is finished and the weather is assessed, I try to decide whether to put some clothes on or be naked or something in between. Sabine is already hard at work on her book as I wander into the sitting room and make myself comfortable on the settee with my laptop to check my emails and to generally see if there is anything new in the world. I am not a morning person and tend to wake up very slowly.

This routine has slight variations, especially if someone else has stayed the night. I find that men are uniformly grumpy in the morning while many women have a tendency to be overly bright and cheerful. I am grateful that neither Sabine nor I are like that. Except for the most basic of greetings, few words are exchanged between us until fairly late in the morning.

At some point during the morning, unless it is pissing with rain, I go for a roundabout stroll through our little naturist village and down to the sea. Of course, during the winter I am snugly bundled up when I go for this ramble but in my mind my body is as free as it is when naked. Seeing the sea seems to invigorate me. I suppose it is that same old thing about feeling a part of nature. It is a similar sensation to staring at the stars on a very clear night. Someone with confidence issues might be tempted to feel a wee bit insignificant.

When I play the piano during the winter, I find that I keep pulling out the sheet music to Gershwin's *Summertime* which I try to perform with a slightly jazzy and languid feel. It is such an evocative piece of music that warms what some people might call their soul. It is also one of the very few songs that I am tempted to sing as I play. A lot of people would consider me to be an excellent pianist but no one would ever applaud me as a singer - not even if I was naked. Luckily, the piano is usually much louder than my voice.

I really think that I should be a better winter naturist - that I should be able to go outside naked when it is cold if only for a little while. One of my male friends suggested that my problem may be that I am fairly thin, that I lack the extra insulation that more hardy naturists seem to possess. He may have just been trying to sweet talk me but it gave me something to think about, not that I would ever consider putting on weight just to feel a bit warmer outside. I am much too obsessive about my weight. But it might be a clue as to why some people can stand the cold better than others.

Two Dutch ice skaters

I think that since Montavilet has much milder winters than Hampshire it would be a good place to experiment with outdoor nudity during the cooler months. After all, it is not necessary to go to Siberia just to be a winter naturist. I have seen several brave individuals around here - usually slightly overweight men - who have been outside wearing nothing more than a pair of hiking boots and thick socks. And men have something to worry about that I do not - shrinkage. So this winter I will definitely be exposing myself to Jacques Frost or, at least, to somewhat colder temperatures than usual.

It might be easier to do that if I had someone to do it with but Sabine just laughed when I made the suggestion. I suppose I could offer to accompany one of the overweight men but I would hate to send out a wrong signal. What I need is a dog that I could take for a walk but I am lumbered with a lazy cat who knows where he is well off. Maybe I could make the suggestion to one of my overnight guests. I suspect the response would be "I'll call you" as they hurry out the door.

Is it really so weird to want to be naked in the winter? Answers on a postcard, please.

Which one is the smart one?

Obviously, it is simply a matter of becoming acclimatized. I need to get used to the cold bit by bit. I will go out onto the patio for just a minute then the next time for a couple of minutes then the time after that I will go slightly farther from the house. Bit by bit, my body will learn to accept the cold. Before long, I will be taking my morning stroll naked – or nearly naked – in December. That, at any rate, is the plan. I have a feeling the first couple of steps will be the hardest.

It is not easy being a compulsive naturist. Perhaps I need analysis but it would probably just turn out to be the old joke - they examined my head but did not find anything. To make matters even more complicated, I am a typical female in that I absolutely love clothes - I just do not want to wear them all the time. And, for a variety of reasons, there are some people who think I look better without clothes.

Naked in London - but is it winter?

When I was a teenager, one of my boyfriends told me that he was of the opinion that girls with bare feet were giving off vibes that they were promiscuous. It was a warm day and I was, of course, running around barefoot. Needless to say, the tactless lad never got to find out if his theory was true - at least, not with me. I wonder what he would think of me now. In fact, I wish I knew where he was so that I could show him what he missed out on. I suppose he eventually got married to a woman who never takes her shoes off. Unless what he really wanted was a barefoot girl. If so, he desperately needed to improve his chat-up lines. One thing I have learned as a naturist - men say the dumbest things.

Every time I read a magazine article or see a television documentary that is supposed to be about naturism, I wish they had talked to me. They always get so much wrong. If only someone would let me make my own documentary about naturism, we might finally get the true picture across to the public who have been, for the most part, woefully misinformed. But perhaps television audiences are not ready for the sight of my naked body on the screen in their sitting rooms.

I never read any books about naturism or nudism before I first took all my clothes off in a public place. It was just something that happened while standing on a beach in the south of France with a few others when someone suggested that we remove our swimsuits just for the hell of it. For the others, it was mostly a bit of a joke and an opportunity to see each other naked. For me, however, it was an epiphany – I felt a sensation that I immediately loved and wanted to feel over and over again. Even today, I had that same marvellous feeling as I slipped off my robe and sat down to write.

To live in a naturist colony like Montavilet is a dream come true even though it is far from perfect and I have to share a villa with someone who is not a lover or even a full-time naturist. I suppose I run the risk of becoming somewhat isolated or insulated in my little naturist environment and could lose touch with the real world if I am not careful. Sabine says that is why she makes frequent trips to Paris - to remind her that there is more to life than living naked (or in her case semi-naked) in Montavilet. But then Sabine has not been a naturist for as long as I have. I like to think I can have the best of both worlds.

This morning I sat naked on my patio for about ten minutes in somewhat hazy sunlight. It was not particularly cold but it was hardly what I would call warm either. Mittens joined me briefly but then scurried back inside. A couple of (clothed) neighbours smiled and waved as they passed by. Sabine poked her head out the door and called me something in French that I had never heard before. I just sat there, reasonably happy that I could indeed feel relatively comfortable being naked in the autumn. Of course, I cheated a little bit - I sat there with one of those large French bowls of hot coffee.

===

SEVEN

Readers of my previous books will know that I have a tendency to fall in love very easily. Well, it has happened again. Her name is Cressida and she is, of course, absolutely fabulous.

I have actually known Cressida for a number of years. She lives in Hampshire not far from my old house and we have a number of mutual friends as well as a shared love of horses. On one of my recent visits back home, I happened to run into her, almost literally, on the High Street in Fordingbridge. We started to chat, we went for a coffee, she invited me to her house for dinner that night, and something clicked. When I asked about her situation, she replied that she was between partners at the moment. For a fairly quiet girl, Cressida had eyes that were full of mischief and temptation. The subject of naturism inevitably came up and she admitted to having tried it a few times on holiday. I told her she should come to Montavilet to enjoy the full experience. She merely smiled in reply.

Cressida is about a year younger than me with a nice body that manages to be both athletic and very feminine. I extended my visit to spend several days with her at her cosy New Forest cottage. She is what we call a woman of independent means thanks to a generous inheritance from her grandmother as well as an even more generous divorce settlement. Since she does not have to work at a "real" job, she keeps busy with various projects and good deeds and also a fair amount of time with her rather sprightly horse Brandywine who I was able to ride. It was so wonderful to be on a horse again but even more wonderful to be with a woman like Cressida and to share the excitement of a brand new affair.

Soon afterwards, Cressida came to stay with me for a week in Montavilet and I was pleasantly surprised by how easily she adapted to the naturist lifestyle. She even managed to get a nod of approval from Sabine not to mention appreciative glances from many of the other residents. Since then, we have made several visits to one another - trying to carry on a long distance friendship that is rather more than just a friendship. I have suggested to Cressida that she could move into my villa but she replied that it would make more sense for me to live with her in

Hampshire. So we remain many miles apart with occasional times spent together. We had a fantastic summer but I am slightly apprehensive about how the winter is going to affect our relationship. I will even admit to being somewhat tempted by Cressida's offer to live with her. Her cottage, like my old house, is sufficiently isolated to permit some warm weather naturism outdoors. However a wet and dreary January in England might well persuade me otherwise. Why does love always have to be so complicated?

In the meantime, life in Montavilet goes on and I will confess to sometimes having other distractions which only serve to confuse matters. It is times like this that I really miss my old gay friend Bryan who was an absolute fountain of wisdom and common sense. We still communicate regularly – mostly by email – but it is not the same as the long and uninhibited late night conversations we used to have when we talked about anything and everything. Even now, from that other world they call California, he is capable of making me smile. Not too long ago, he sent me a t-shirt. I thought it was an odd gift to send to a confirmed naturist until I saw what was printed on it in big bold letters: "Nudist On Strike".

I know that I have always insisted that sex and naturism are two entirely different things that only occasionally connect but there are times when it is virtually impossible to look at other naked bodies with more than merely aesthetic appreciation. It may disappoint some male readers to learn that quite a few naturist women tend to look at other women's bodies more than men's. It has nothing to do with lesbianism or bisexuality - it is simply that the female body is so much nicer to view. Whether there is any subconscious or even repressed lust is involved is questionable but a lack of clothing does sometimes also lead to a loss of other inhibitions.

It would seem fairly certain that those people who go naked when there is snow and ice on the ground are doing it for reasons that have nothing to do with sex. It is probably another way to experience that feeling of freedom that most people would prefer to feel in much warmer weather. But naturism should not be restricted to just a few months of the year - at least, not for those of us for whom being naked is more of a lifestyle than a hobby. I just wish my little body did not hate being cold so much.

I am beginning to think that being naked in winter, for me at least, is a case of seizing an opportunity when it presents itself but otherwise trying to stay warm while impatiently waiting for the warm sun of spring and summer to return. In other words, I will simply have to do what I have always done – muddle through the winter and find something else to do to take my mind off the weather. Perhaps the internet could empty my mind for a few months or maybe I could write a real book, a novel all about this girl who…um…erm…it will come to me. Maybe I will just take another stab at reading *War and Peace*.

I think that one of the things I hate most about winter is how short the days are – that terribly depressing period between the Autumn Equinox in September and the Winter Solstice in December when the sun sets earlier and earlier each day until soon it is dark before dinner time. The changing of the clocks in October does not help matters either. I find myself putting on every light in the house in an attempt to improve the atmosphere of the place. I probably get through more bottles of wine during the winter as well.

Not even chilly weather can completely diminish the joy of being naked. It is such a simple thing - to take my clothes off - yet it produces such a liberating and relaxing feeling over my entire being. I know that some of the people who read my books are dedicated naturists but there are also a number of very curious readers as well. If you have ever thought about being a nudist, why not try it on your own in the privacy of your own home. It is a very good way to start. Just take your clothes off and then do what you would normally do around the house - except you will be doing it naked. You may momentarily feel slightly nervous or even guilty but very soon that marvellous feeling of freedom will kick in and you will discover for yourself what I have been talking about. Be naked - be free - be happy!

Of course, if you have a good friend or a loved one to share the sensation with, so much the better. Private naturism can be pleasant but shared nudity is so much nicer. I suppose I have been fortunate to have had people who enjoyed being naked with me, beginning with my sister. This is not always the case. Sometimes even a joking suggestion to try naturism can lead to accusations of mental illness or sexual depravity. I know one family where the husband is an ardent nudist, mostly at home, but his wife and daughters have no desire to participate. Instead, they tolerate his nudity which is really all a naturist wants – tolerance. When I first started to go naked on beaches as a teenager, my mother was convinced that it was merely a phase I was going through. Twenty years later and I am still going through that phase with no end in sight. Well, one end if you count my little bottom.

It is very late at night and I am sitting here in my big fluffy dressing gown and a pair of socks but I would much rather be naked. So – off they come. At first there is a slight chill that gives me goosies all over and makes my nipples stand up but that is a small price to pay for being naked with friends. Maybe this winter will not be so bad after all.

I seem to have reached the age where I am becoming nostalgic. At night, I lie in bed and my thoughts are equally divided between things I have done in my life and things I still want to do. There is very little in the past that I truly regret and I am full of optimism for the future. I better start taking care of this body if I still want to be a naturist at seventy. Now there is an ambition – one I fully expect to achieve.

===

ABOUT THE AUTHOR

Sally Dali is the pen name of a thirty-seven year old English naturist who has enjoyed the lifestyle for more than twenty years. Her first book, *Being Naked*, was an honest recollection of her experiences. This was followed by *Still Naked*, a continuation of her story mixed with some thoughts and philosophy about naturism. She has also written a collection of short stories with a nudist theme called *Naked People*. Sally currently divides her time between several addresses in southern England and the naturist resort of Montavilet in France.

Printed in Great Britain
by Amazon.co.uk, Ltd.,
Marston Gate.